CONTENTS

Where food comes from

What do you like for breakfast?

Milk, cereal and fruit are

favourite breakfast foods.

How does this food get

from farms to shop shelves?

The food we eat is grown
on farms. Farmers plant and grow
crops and fruit. Livestock farmers
raise animals for meat or eggs.

Collecting milk

Dairy farmers raise cows for milk. The farmers use machines to get the milk from the cows.

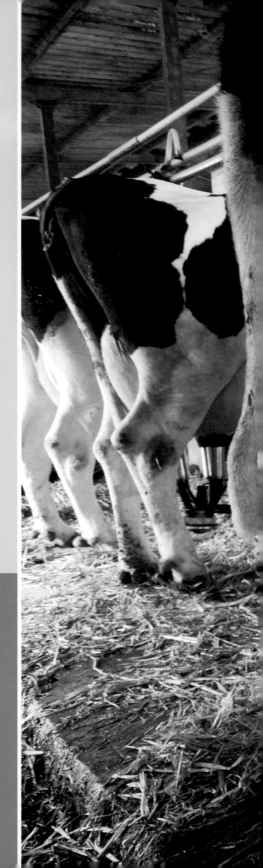

milking machine

Milk is collected in tanker lorries.
It is processed and packaged
into containers. Lorries deliver
the containers to shops.

tanker lorry

11

Making cereal

Farmers harvest crops

when they are ripe.

Lorries take corn, oats, wheat

and other types of grain to mills.

The grain is turned into flour.

Food companies buy the flour
to make their products.
Breakfast cereal is made
from cereal grain flour.

bags of flour

Cereal is packaged into boxes.
Workers load them onto lorries.
Lorry drivers deliver the boxes
to shops.

toaster pastries
granola bars
pancake/syrup
cereal
hot cereal
coffee

pasta
pasta sauce
boxed pasta
juice

Travelling far

Bananas and other types of fruit
may come from far away.
They are picked, boxed and loaded
onto ships. They travel across oceans.
Then lorries take the fruit to shops.

Working together

Farmers grow our food.

Lorry drivers deliver it to shops.

Shop assistants put it on the shelves.

Many people work together

to get our food from here to there.

GLOSSARY

crop   plant that farmers grow in large amounts, usually for food

dairy farm   farm where cows are raised for their milk

grain   seed of a cereal plant such as wheat, rice, corn, oat or barley

harvest   gather crops that are ripe

livestock   animals that are raised for their meat, eggs or milk

mill   building that has machines to grind grain into flour

package   place into plastic containers, cartons or boxes

process   put through a series of steps; milk is processed so that it is safe to drink and ready to be sold in shops

BOOKS

Combine Harvesters, Hannah Wilson (Kingfisher, 2015)

Farming (Geography Detective Investigates), Jen Green, Wayland, 2013

Food from Farmers series, Ruth Owen (Windmill Books, 2012)

From Farm to Table (Food and Farming), Richard Spilsbury (Powerkids Press, 2010)

WEBSITES

www.bbc.co.uk/gardening/gardening_with_children/
didyouknow_cereals.shtml
Find out about cereal plants on this site.

www.foodafactoflife.org.uk/Activity.aspx?contentId=174&
sectionId=63&siteId=14
This site has activities to help you learn where food
comes from.

www.theschoolrun.com/homework-help/food-and-farming
This site has lots of fascinating facts about food and where
it comes from.

CRITICAL THINKING QUESTIONS

1. What would happen if farmers stopped growing grain?

2. Describe the trip milk takes to get to a shop.

INDEX